Havering
in old picture postcards

by Andrew Brooks

European Library ZALTBOMMEL/THE NETHERLANDS

Cover picture
Hornchurch Windmill in 1909
with a cart loaded up with flour.
There were three corn-mills in
Hornchurch in the Middle Ages.
Two of them had gone by the 18th
century. This mill, which was
rebuilt in the 17th century, stood
on a site of mills going back at least
to 1262. It continued in use until
1912.

BACK IN TIME

GB ISBN 90 288 6484 9

© 1997 European Library – Zaltbommel/The Netherlands

Introduction

On 1st April 1965 the London Borough of Havering was established as part of the new Greater London Council. The new borough on the semi-rural eastern fringe of Greater London united two Essex towns and a number of former villages under the ancient name of Havering.

The Greater London Council is no more; the victim of later local government reforms. But the new boroughs created in 1965 carry on, like Havering, with their own distinct character and charm. Havering embraces two south Essex towns, Romford and Hornchurch, together with the villages of Cranham, Great Warley, North Ockendon, Rainham, Upminster and Wennington. Some twelve-and-a-half miles from central London the borough covers an area of forty-six square miles from the River Thames to Hainault Forest.

Though parts of Havering still retain their old rural air, the borough is more noted for the bustle of Romford Market and the swathes of residential estates built over the past sixty years for commuters attracted by the fast train services to London. But the history of Havering begins with a road, the mighty Roman road which ran from London to Colchester and crossed the river we now call the Rom at Romford. Stone Age men roamed Havering and relics going back to the Bronze Age have been found in the area which in Roman days was called 'Durolitum', a Celtic word meaning 'the fort by the ford'.

Roman rule lasted for four hundred years but it left little trace in Havering apart from that road. A burial pot found in Romford implies the site of a Roman cemetery by the road and we know there was a villa at Collier Row. Perhaps Oldchurch, just south of Romford Market, marks the site of 'Durolitum' on the grounds that in the 17th century six fields were called ruin meadow, lower ruins, great ruins and three little ruins.

The Romans were replaced by Saxon chiefs, who came from Holland and Germany to help the local Celtic kings in their wars and stayed as conquerors to found kingdoms of their own.

The East Saxons established a kingdom in the 6th century which survived for over three hundred years. The county of Essex still bears their name and many towns and villages preserve the names of local Saxon leaders and their followers.

In the Middle Ages a quaint legend linked Havering with the great Saxon king Edward the Confessor, who became King of England in 1042. According to a story which goes back at least to the 12th century, Edward was attending the consecration of a local church when an old beggar asked him for alms in the name of God and St. John. Edward's purse was empty, so the saintly king gave the old man a ring from his finger. Some years later two pilgrims coming from the Holy Land returned the ring which had been given to them by the old man who turned out to be St. John the Evangelist himself. And that's how Havering (Have a Ring) got it's name and why a ring features on the modern borough's coat of arms!

A more mundane explanation is that Havering, or 'Haveringas' as it was first known, owes its name to an early East Saxon warrior called Haefer and simply means the settlement of Haefer's people. It was also said that nightingales had disturbed Edward the Confessor at his devotions and so he prayed for them to go away and they never returned to disturb him in Havering.

Edward's successor, Harold Godwinson, held the Manor of Havering until his death in 1066 at the Battle of Hastings. But his name is remembered in Harold Wood to this day and in the new estate of Harold Hill.

Later kings stayed in Havering at their palace or bower and the village was called Havering-atte-Bower. The villagers who worked on this Royal Manor were granted special privileges, set out in the famous charter of 1465, which created the Royal Liberty of Havering. These grants, customs and courts were not finally abolished until 1892.

The 'capital' of the Manor was Romford with its busy markets, but the parish church was in Hornchurch in the south of the modern borough. The palace has long gone. During the Civil War it was taken over by parliamentary forces, the Royal Park was sold and the palace abandoned. By the 18th century it had fallen into ruins and by 1816 nothing was left of the great house. Romford, whose name means 'roomy ford', grew up along the Roman road which the Saxons called 'here strete' or 'army street' after the legions they supposed had built it. Today its course is still marked by Romford's Hare Street.

It was an ideal site for a market, which began in 1247 and continues to this day. Though its character has changed the Market Place remains a centre for buying and selling. The cattle and livestock market was closed in 1958, but a brisk trade continues in the fruit, vegetables, fresh meat and fish. Other stalls stock clothes and electrical goods in furious competition with the big stores, arcades and shopping malls which have sprung up over the last forty years around the market centre.

People travel far and wide to shop in Romford. Shoppers from eastern London and south Essex will rub shoulders with visitors from Belgium on shopping spree coach trips on market days. All will be looking for choice, quality and value for money in the shops or on the stalls.

If Romford is noise and bustle the south of the borough is an oasis of suburban calm. Hornchurch, with its famous medieval church, is now a major residential area, but the farms of the outlying areas to the south and west preserve Havering's old ties with the Essex countryside.

This selection of postcards covers the period of transition over the past hundred years. Rural districts become housing estates, quiet lanes become busy thoroughfares. They were the 'good old days' of our grandfathers' memories. Those days may not have been all that rosy, but they are certainly gone for good.

Acknowledgements:

I would like to thank Stephen Pewsey for his help and encouragement in the production of this book and Eclipse Archive for access to their collection of postcards.

1 Havering-atte-Bower Church

The Church of St. John the Evangelist was consecrated in 1878 on the site of an earlier church, which had been one of the chapels of the old royal palace.

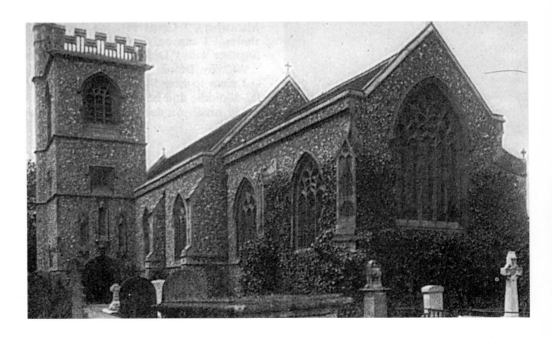

2 St. Andrew's Church, Hornchurch in 1905

The church stands on a hill and the spire was used as a navigational aid by ships on the Thames. Trinity House contributed to its repair. This is the 'Horned Church' that gave the village its name. A stone head of a bull with a pair of copper horns hangs from the eastern gable. The name goes back to at least the 13th century, but the original meaning of the tradition has been long forgotten. Some believe it is linked with the local cattle trade – others more fancifully suggest that the church lies on the site of a pagan temple and the horns are a memory of pre-Christian rituals.

3 St. Andrew's Church, Romford before the First World War

Romford Barracks was built during the Napoleonic Wars for six troops of cavalry. It was demolished in 1825 and the site developed for industrial use and housing for the workers. St. Andrew's was built in 1862 to meet the needs of the new housing estate. The Victorian artisans' cottages have now been replaced by council flats.

St. Andrew's Church. — Romford.

4 The Bell Inn and St. Laurence Church, Upminster

Though the tower goes back to the 13th century the rest of the church was virtually rebuilt in Victorian days. The Bell Inn dates back to 1769 and was demolished in 1962.

H.11   THE BELL INN & ST. LAURENCE CHURCH, UPMINSTER.

5 All Saints, Cranham

A church had stood here since the 13th century, but it was completely rebuilt in 1873. The founder of the American State of Georgia, General James Oglethorpe, died here in 1785 and is buried in the churchyard.

6 Salem Baptist Chapel, Romford

The Salem Church in London Road was founded in 1836. This yellow-brick building was opened in 1847 for the growing congregation. Though the chapel can seat four hundred, there were only 54 members in 1850. But the church soon witnessed rapid growth, due partly to the work of outstanding local members like John Rootsey Ward.

7 The Hall, Havering in 1905

This large, double-fronted three-storeyed Victorian mansion was built in 1858. It was damaged by fire in the Thirties and was partially demolished in 1976.

The Hall, Havering.

8 The Bower House, Havering

This house was built in 1729 using bricks and stones taken from the old royal palace at Havering. But it had its share of royal visitors. In 1801 the six year old Princess Charlotte stopped over on her way back from a holiday at Southend. Queen Mary also was a guest in 1934. The building is now used by the Ford Motor Company.

THE BOWER HOUSE, HAVERING-ATTE-BOWER.

9 Round House, Havering in 1905

But it's really oval not round! It was said that it was modelled on a tea-caddy in the 1790s for the tea merchant who owned it. But it is now largely known for being the home of a noted rosegrower, the Rev. J.H. Pemberton, who propagated the Alexandra Rose, named in honour of Queen Alexandra. He was curate of the Church of the Ascension from 1880 to 1923.

Havering, Round House.

10 Fairkytes, Hornchurch in 1910

Another old house first recorded in 1520. This building was erected in the mid-18th century and refronted and enlarged in the Victorian era. It housed the public library from 1953 to 1967 and it's been the home of the Havering Art Centre since 1976.

11 Langton's Gardens, Hornchurch about 1960

Langtons was built in the early 18th century on the site of a manor house first recorded in 1446. It was given to the local council in 1929 on the condition that they should preserve the mansion and its gardens. The garden is a public park and the house was used as council offices until 1965. Langtons now serves as the office of the superintendent registrar for Havering.

Langtons Gardens, Hornchurch   No. 2324

12 Lodge Gates, Grey Towers, before the First World War

Grey Towers was built in 1876 for Henry Holmes, the Hornchurch brewer. This Victorian 'castle' stood in a 50 acre park in Hornchurch Road and was the last country house built in Hornchurch. It was used as a barracks during the First World War and it was finally demolished in 1931.

Lodge Gates, Hornchurch.

13 Dagnam Park, Harold Hill in 1810

'Dagnam' is in fact Dagenham
– the name of a nearby village
to the west – and it accurately
reflects a local accent only
now dying out. In the Middle
Ages two large, adjoining
estates were held by Roger
Cockerel and Thomas of
Dagenham and the land was
later called the manor of
Dagenhams and Cockerels.
This great house was built for
Sir Richard Neave, who
bought the manor in 1772.
His descendants lived in it
until the Second World War.
Dagnam Park was sold in
1948 for housing develop-
ment and the mansion was
pulled down.

14 Dagnam Park Farm, Harold Hill

This 17th century farm-house was known as Cockerels House until the 19th century. It too was demolished in 1948.

Dagnam Park Farm, Harold Park.

15 Gidea Hall, Romford in 1637

This engraving depicts the departure of Marie de Medici together with her son-in-law King Charles I from the mansion called Gidea Hall. A hall stood here from at least the 13th century. The estate was later owned by Sir Thomas Cooke, a draper who became Lord Mayor of London in 1462. One of his descendants was Sir Anthony Cooke, the tutor to Edward VI. Sir Anthony's children were so learned that a visitor compared Gidea Hall to a university.

16 Gidea Hall in 1730

Old Gidea Hall was demolished in 1720, though part of the stables survived until 1922. This engraving, by the local artist and landscape architect Humphry Repton, shows the new mansion which replaced it. Repton may have planned the grounds for the new house. During the First World War it was used as a barracks for the Artist's Rifles, a volunteer corps founded in 1859 by an art student, Edward Sterling. Its last use was as a clubhouse for the new Gidea Park housing estate built on the old grounds. The building was finally demolished in 1930.

17 Upminster Court, Upminster

This splendid Edwardian mansion was built in 1905. It was bought in 1945 by Essex County Council for use as the education office of the South Essex Division. It later housed the offices of the Havering education department.

18 Upminster Hall, Upminster

Upminster Hall manor goes back to late Saxon days, when it was given by Harold Godwinson to Waltham Abbey in 1062. Waltham Abbey held the manor until the dissolution of the monasteries during the Reformation. This timber-framed building is certainly 16th century and parts may even be a century older. It is now the clubhouse of Upminster Golf Club.

19 Romford Brewery

Romford is famous for its beer and this is the modern bottling plant of the well-known Ind Coope Brewery.

20 Ind Coope Brewery in 1908

The brewery was on a prime site very near to Romford railway station. When this photo was taken the company employed 450 workers. You can see the brewery's own railway sidings which linked to the station. Look at the stacked barrels on the right and the River Rom emerging under the bridges.

21 Victoria Flour Mills, Romford

This steam flour mill in Victoria Road was built in 1858 as the sign on the gable proudly proclaims. Henry Whitmore bought it in 1874. The mill, like the horse-drawn carriages drawn in front, are no more. It was closed in 1928 and pulled down two years later.

22 Hornchurch Windmill

A postcard of the mill some
years after its closure in 1912.
It was destroyed in a fire in
1921.

23 The Bell Hotel, Upminster in 1908

The original Bell Inn was built in 1769. The inn was later rebuilt some 40 yards away on part of the former village green. It was demolished in 1962.

24 The Orange Tree, Romford

This photo taken around 1900 seems to transport us to a world without cars. It is, in fact, a careful and sentimental composition of the camera-man. Note the two bicycles, 'casually' placed on either side of the road, and the mysterious horse and cart by the rider.

25 William Derham
(1657-1735)

Dr. Derham was rector of
Upminster Church from
1689 to 1735. A noted the-
ologian and natural scientist
of his day he lived at High
House, opposite the church
in Corbets Tey Road.

Engrav'd by Jos.ᵇ Baker.

26 The notorious Colonel Blood

Colonel Thomas Blood has gone down in history as the only man to succeed in stealing the Crown Jewels from the Tower of London. He lived in an apothecary's house in the Market Place in Romford. In 1668 he freed a friend from prison with the help of three accomplices. They then raided the Tower – but not without bloodshed. He was wounded five times but managed to escape to Romford. Some believe that the spendthrift Charles II was part of a plot to steal his own Crown. In any case, the King pardoned Blood, who died in 1680 on a royal pension.

Blood & his Accomplices making their Escape after Stealing the Crown from the TOWER of LONDON.

Lodge Sculp.

27 The Goat-Woman of Havering-atte-Bower

Elizabeth Balls was born in Hertfordshire in 1760. Jilted by her sweetheart she vowed to leave home and her father bought her a cottage on Havering green. There she shunned all human company but gave open house to all sorts of stray animals – cats and dogs, chickens, sheep and some fifty goats! Soon her fame reached London society and it became a fad to come and see the 'Goat Woman'. After her death in 1823 the animals were sold and the cottage was pulled down.

28 Edward Ind the brewer

Edward Ind bought the Star Inn in 1799. A small brewery by the river Rom in the High Street was attached to the tavern. In 1845 Octavius and George Coope became partners in a business which has gone from strength to strength.

29 John Rootsey Ward

Romford's Baptists founded their Salem church in 1836. With just thirteen members they met in John Rootsey Ward's school in the Market Place. He devoted his life to the Baptist church. His school closed in 1845 and J.R. Ward turned to the commercial world becoming an insurance agent for the Essex Provident Society and later a clerk to the Savings Bank. He never married and lived modestly until his death in 1868.

30 Walter Southgate

The Labour historian and
founder of the National
Museum of Labour History
lived in Romford.

31 E.A. Hillman with his Rolls Royce at Maylands Aerodrome

Edward Hillman was a local transport king, whose coach business grew from one vehicle in 1928 to the second largest fleet in the country by 1932. In 1931 he took over the licence at Maylands Aerodrome at Harold Wood to launch an air wing to his coach empire. Hillman's Airways Ltd. was founded in 1933 with routes all over Britain and one to Paris. Hillman died in 1934 and his airline merged with United Airways and Spartan Air Lines in 1935.

32 Swimming Baths and Central Park, Harold Hill about 1965

Harold Godwinson – the ill-fated King Harold who lost his crown and life to William the Conqueror in 1066 – held the Manor of Havering. Havering was well-wooded in the Middle Ages and one of them, Harold Wood, preserved the name of its last Saxon lord. When the London County Council bought the land after the Second World War to rehouse Londoners, the name was changed to Harold Hill.

SWIMMING BATH & CENTRAL PARK, HAROLD HILL.   H.H.S.

33 Harold Hill Community Centre about 1965

The London County Council built some 8,200 houses and several factories on the former Dagnam Park estate. Worked started in 1948 and continued for the next ten years.

HAROLD HILL COMMUNITY CENTRE.   H.H.6.

34 Harold Hill Community Centre about 1965

Centres like this provided venues for local societies, political parties as well as weddings and bazaars.

HAROLD HILL COMMUNITY CENTRE.   H.H.7.

35 Council Schools, Hornchurch

A school board was established in Hornchurch in 1889 which immediately took over four existing schools and built two more. Essex County Council built six primary and five secondary schools between 1929 and 1939.

36 South Street, Romford in 1908

Another view of old Romford. The old man on the left is unloading milk pails.

37 Roome's Department Store, Grand Opening 1937

James Roome opened a small drapery and haberdashery shop in Upton Park in 1888. The family lived in Upminster and in 1927 his son M. B. Roome opened a small shop in Station Road, Upminster. In 1935 he decided to close the Upton Park shop and concentrate on the Upminster business. The new store, aimed at the new populaton who had moved into the new housing built after the First World War, was opened on the site of his old shop in 1937.

38 'The Market' Upminster about 1908

Though the railway had opened in 1885 Upminster remained a quiet backwater because the major landowners initially refused to sell their land. But it all changed at the turn of the century when housing developers bought land for private houses near the station. This parade was built to meet the needs of the new commuters drawn to the village by the quality of the housing and the speed of the train.

39 Harrow Lodge Park, Hornchurch about 1965

Harrow Lodge was built in 1787 and it was used as a public library from 1936 to 1967. The River Ravensbourne runs through the 120 acre park, which is the largest in Hornchurch.

HARROW LODGE PARK, HORNCHURCH.

H.7

40 Hylands Recreation Ground, Hornchurch

A small oasis of calm in a modern estate.

HYLANDS RECREATION GROUND, HORNCHURCH.

41 Central Park, Harold Hill about 1965

Parks, swings and paddling pools were the stuff of most Romford childhoods in the Fifties and Sixties.

CENTRAL PARK, HAROLD HILL.   H.H.8

42 Dagnam Park, Harold Hill about 1965

When the LCC estate was built on the old Dagnam Park grounds two large areas of park-land were retained as public parks.

DAGNAM PARK HAROLD HILL. H.H.4

43 North Hill Recreation Ground, Harold Hill about 1965

Another part of the old Dagnam Park grounds converted into a public park in the new Harold Hill residential estate.

NORTH HILL RECREATION GROUND, HAROLD HILL. H.H.10.

44   Clock House Lake and Gardens, Upminster

The Clock House was originally the stable-block of New Place House, a manor-house rebuilt in the 18th century and pulled down in 1924. The clock, which long provided the time for the village, came from Woolwich Arsenal. The Clock House was used for council offices from 1924 to 1934 and was used as a branch of Hornchurch public library from 1936 to 1963.

CLOCK HOUSE LAKE AND GARDENS, UPMINSTER   L 2128

45 Upminster Recreation Ground about 1965

The first park in Upminster was on land rented by the parish council in 1899. When this was reclaimed to site a golf-course in 1928 the council bought some land near the church and established Upminster Park. Upminster Hall playing fields were laid out in 1962.

UPMINSTER RECREATION GROUND.

H.10

**46   R.W. Beard's team at
Hampden FC Ground,
Collier Row Lane**

R.W. Beard was a local
Hornchurch baker. This photo
was taken on 11th April
1937.

47 The Stocks, Havering-atte-Bower about 1905

The days when justice was literally seen to be done had long gone, even when this photo was taken. The stocks and whipping post on the village green still stand today as a memento of a harsher time.

The Stocks, Havering.

48 Havering Village in 1905

From a time when the horse
was still the king. A common
enough scene in Essex at the
time, but one which was to
vanish quicker than anyone
could imagine as the 20th
century moved on.

Entrance to Havering Village.

49 The Church and Dell, Hornchurch

The natural arena behind St. Andrew's was probably the result of ancient quarrying. Long known as the Dell it was used for village sports in the 18th and 19th century. In 1795 Daniel Mendoza, the Jewish boxer, came to the Dell to defend his heavyweight title against 'Gentleman' John Jackson. Over 3,000 spectators packed the Dell to see Jackson defeat Mendoza in nine rounds.

The Church & Dell — Hornchurch

H. Luff, Hornchurch, Essex.

50 High Street Hornchurch in 1904

Note the saddler's shop on the right and the absence of any street lighting.

51 High Street Hornchurch in 1909

The Bull Inn on the right went back to the 16th century, with considerable enlargement in the 1700s. It was rebuilt in 1953.

52 Hornchurch village, 1908

Another picture of rural charm. The house on the right is weather-boarded with elm planking in the traditional south Essex style. This was the centre of the old village. All the old houses were swept away long ago.

53 Romford Market Place looking towards Laurie Hall about 1900

The market, which was licensed by Henry III in 1247, is the heart of the town. Like most country markets it was a centre for the trade in cattle, pigs and farm produce for centuries. The market belonged to the Lords of the Manor of Havering until it was sold to the local council in 1892. Stone's Store, in the far right of the photograph, took over these market premises in 1892.

54 Laurie Hall on Market Day, Romford about 1900

Cattle are being taken down for sale by Laurie Hall, which was built in 1847 on the site of the town stocks. Dickens and Thackeray gave readings in the Hall. James Finley used the top floor for his un-denominational and temperance Christian mission from 1895. You can see his slogan 'Preach Christ' along the pediment. Laurie Hall was converted into a cinema in 1913. The hall was demolished in 1970.

55 Romford Market about 1964

The cattle market was closed in 1958, but the stall traders carried on and the market continued to grow. Today private traffic is barred on market days and stalls flank both sides of the road.

ROMFORD MARKET

535

56 Romford High Street

A turn of the century photo taken during a quiet day in Romford.

Romford, High Street.

57 North Street, Romford in 1955

The beginnings of the post-war boom can be seen in the new buildings on either side of the road.

ROMFORD, NORTH STREET.

V.1266

58 Main Road, Gidea Park, about 1955

The Gidea Hall estate was sold for development in 1897. Part of it became a public park and a golf course. The rest was reserved for the Gidea Park garden suburb and the first houses built in 1911. Gidea Park never developed in the way it was originally foreseen and the garden suburb idea was dropped in the Thirties in favour of more piece-meal development.

MAIN ROAD, GIDEA PARK

59 Petersfield Avenue, Harold Hill about 1955

Harold Hill grew after the Second World War, when the London County Council developed the land to provide more homes for Londoners. Some 8,200 houses and some factories were built by the LCC in Harold Hill from 1948 to 1958.

PETERSFIELD AVENUE, HAROLD HILL. H.H.9.

60 Birds Lane Corner, Upminster in 1909

An idyllic pastoral scene from an age still within living memory. Today traffic on the busy Southend arterial road roars past this site.

61 Yew Avenue, Upminster about 1900

Another Upminster view of rural peace now sadly gone.

59866.

YEW AVENUE, UPMINSTER, AT THE TURN OF THE CENTURY.

62 Noak Hill, Romford Road around 1900

The name of this village in the north of the borough simply meant 'at the oak' hill in the Middle Ages. Though this view gives the impression that nothing had changed for hundreds of years, the telegraph lines on the left show the beginnings of the modern age.

Noak Hill, Romford Road.

63 Hornchurch Station looking east

Hornchurch railway station was opened in 1885 for the London, Tilbury and Southend line from Barking to Upminster. In 1902 London Underground's District Railway used the station for its own service to Upminster and Southend. The station was run by the nationalised British Railways Board until the 1970s. By then it was exclusively used by London Underground's District Line, which continues the service today.

64 Romford Station in 1908

Romford Station was opened in 1839 for the Eastern Counties railway line to London. The line was extended to Brentwood in 1840 and a service was runnning to Colchester by 1847. In 1862 it became, as part of a general amalgamation, part of the Great Eastern Railway. The express run from London's Liverpool Street took just 22 minutes in 1912.

65 Romford Station, South Street

This view taken from the High Street shows the main entrance to the Great Eastern railway station on the right and the entrance to the separate LTS station on the left. The LTS station was built in 1893 for their branch line to Upminster. The stations were combined in 1934 and the old LTS entrance and booking hall converted into shops.

Romford Station.

66 *St. Pancras* steaming towards Upminster

This is a fine shot of LTS loco No. 31 on its way to Southend. The London, Tilbury and Southend railway became part of the Midland Railway in 1912, which in turn merged to become the London, Midland and Scottish Railway in 1923.

67 Upminster Station, August 1926

This LTS station was opened in 1885. By 1926 it was part of the mighty London, Midland, Scottish network. We are looking at LMS loco 2175, formerly LTS *Mark Lane* and built in 1903. The District Railway started using the station in 1902 for their own London service, but regular Underground services began after electrification in 1932. Upminster today is the District line's eastern terminus and a key station on the main line London Fenchurch Street to Southend service.

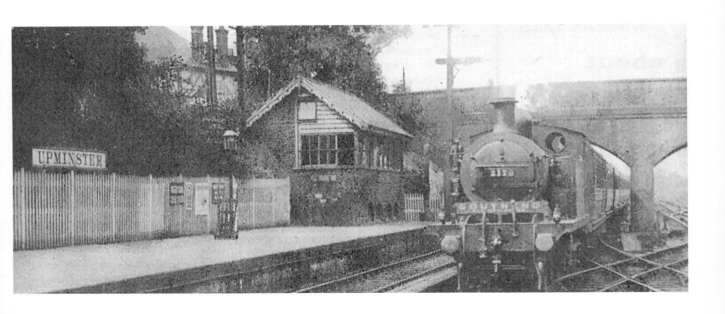

68 Signal box, Cranham Woods in 1925

This cabin controlled the sidings of Cranham Brickfield. The Cranham Brick and Tile Co. opened a kiln in 1900 and carried on until 1920. Cranham Woods are in the background.

Cranham Woods   104651

69 Beam Bridge Lock, Romford Canal, Hornchurch in 1937

Throughout the 19th century plans were drawn for a canal to link Romford with Thames. Between 1875 and 1880 work was started by the Romford Canal Company. The company ran out of money and was wound up in 1882 with the project barely begun. Some three miles were constructed, but none of it was ever opened. In 1912 the land was sold by auction by the Bank of England. Even this lock was unfinished. This stretch of the canal has now been filled in.

70 A Hillman coach in Romford Market

Edward Hillman started his coach company in 1928 with just one coach, a Gilford like the one in this photo. Based in Stratford, his first route ran from Stratford to Romford and Brentwood. By 1930 the Hillmans Saloon Coaches fleet ran to 57 coaches taking people to London, and throughout East Anglia. The head office was in Romford and Hillman lived in Gidea Park in a house named 'Gilford', painted in his company's colours – blue and white.

71 Works outing from Maylands Aerodrome in 1932

Edward Hillman also pioneered regional air travel. These Edwards & Co. workers are flying on Hillman's Airways to Clacton. Two years later it was all over. In January 1934 the new London Passenger Transport Board took over most of his coach routes. He sold the rest of the coach business off in August and died suddenly on the last day of the year at the age of 45. Some say of a broken heart.

72 Sutton's Farm Aerodrome Hornchurch in the First World War

The Royal Flying Corps airfield at Sutton's farm was opened in 1915 to defend London from German airships. The first three German Zeppelin airships to be shot down fell victim to pilots from the aerodrome. This photo shows Lt. Frederick Sowrey in his BE2c fighter, which destroyed the German L32 airship in 1916.

73 Entrance to Grey Towers Barracks in 1915

War broke out in August 1914 and men from all over Britain responded to the call for volunteers for the Army.

Romford was no exception and the town was soon full of soldiers. Grey Towers mansion became an army camp for the Sportmen's Battalion in November 1914, soon after the outbreak of war, and it continued to house troops until the end of hostilities.

74 William Leefe-Robinson VC

Flight Lt. William Leefe-Robinson became an overnight hero in 1916 when he became the first man to shoot down a German airship. He scrambled from Hornchurch aerodrome and half London watched as he blew the SL-11 out of the night sky. The wreckage fell to earth at Cuffley, Herts., and Leefe-Robinson won the Victoria Cross. Later captured over France, he was released in 1918, but died of influenza in the same year.

75 RAF Boulton-Paul Defiants at Hornchurch Aerodrome 1940

Sutton's farm aerodrome was closed in 1919 but re-opened in 1924. The Second World War broke out in 1939 and Hornchurch's airmen played a heroic role in the Battle of France and Battle of Britain and throughout the war. Hornchurch fighters may have accounted for over five hundred German aircraft. Their own losses amounted to 132. This shot is of a two-seater fighter designed as a bomber escort which began operations in 1940.

76 Gloster Green, Suttons Lane

The war ended in victory in 1945, but flying had ceased at RAF Hornchurch a year earlier. The station was retained by the RAF until 1963, when the land was sold for development – much of it new housing like this.